Coffee, Baileys, and Corona – A Veteran's Guide Through the Pandemic Highway

WCP Publishing

<<<>>>

Fort Worth, Texas

Printed in the United States of America

Paxton, Guillermo

Coffee, Baileys, and Corona – A Veteran's Guide Through the
Pandemic Highway/Paxton – 1st Edition

ISBN: 978-0-9771993-5-8

1. Coffee, Baileys, and Corona – A Veteran's Guide Through the
Pandemic Highway – Humor – Non-Fiction.

WCP Publishing – Non-Fiction.

Dedicated to my fellow veterans, especially to those that
gave all- we, the living, have a duty to those that are no
longer with us to live our lives like they would were they
given that chance

If you think that breakfast is a shot of Jim Beam with a beer chaser, you might be a veteran.

If you remember having jungle juice but not much after that, you might be a veteran.

If you refer to your spouse as a "good piece of gear", you just might be a veteran.

If you refer to your reading glasses as "birth-control glasses", you're probably a veteran.

If you know what the "chair force" is, you might be a veteran.

If you're about to go on a cruise in six days and a wake up, you might just be a veteran.

If you've ever "field-stripped" one of your kid's toys, you're definitely a veteran.

Preface-

What is truly sad about our current political and social climate is that I've even considered not publishing this book. It was brief, albeit, but a thought, nevertheless.

I have friends and family that I respect and care for that think very differently than I do politically. I'm not here to defend nor propagate my political and social views. The last few years have been hard for many people. Isolation, depression, and an unhealthy dose of the 24-hour news cycle, have all contributed to the creation of this book. Not to depress you, but to entertain you. Maybe you are a person that stayed locked up in your house since March of 2020. Maybe you're still in lock-down mode. Maybe you are like me and my wife and you lived life as normally as was humanly possible during this crazy time. Whatever type of person that you are, whatever your background might be, whatever gender you are, no matter your political or sexual orientation, I invite you to read this book the way you might have read a book back in 2010. So what if we don't agree?

If you are unable to set aside all of those angry emotions that have been so readily exploited for the last several years, you probably should not buy or read this short book. While it is meant to entertain you, and give people an insight on to how we personally dealt with the pandemic, I do not wish for it to become some negative in your life.

My wife and I are veterans. We love our country, regardless of its imperfections and difficult history. We believe in debate and opposing viewpoints and that off-color humor is still funny and if you are easily offended then you should probably stay home and disconnect from all technology.

Chapter One- Breakfast and Baileys

Pandemic Rule #1 - Start every day with a nutritional breakfast

Well, if you're reading this, you're either reading the little preview given on Amazon, or you actually bought the book. If you haven't bought the book, get off your indecisive little ass, support a veteran, and buy it you cheapskate! If you did buy it, well, you're here now, so you might as well read it. And thanks, by the way, it's really tough being broke in the pandemic, or any other time for that matter, and I need beer money. No, really, I thank you. Which brings me to breakfast.

A few years ago, I discovered Baileys and coffee. I don't know why it took me that long to find out about the pair, but it changed my life. Seriously, it was a nearly religious experience for me. When I think of all the wasted years drinking half-and-half in my coffee, it's tough holding back the tears. I used to have eggs and chorizo for breakfast; now, I have a 32-ounce Yeti of coffee and a Baileys facsimile. What do you mean it isn't really Baileys? No, I'm a disabled veteran, bro. I drink knock offs. Baileys is amazing, but it's too damn expensive to drink for breakfast every day.

Sunday, I woke up and stumbled down the poorly carpeted stairs to make my morning cup of coffee – and no fucking way, we were out of our Bailey's facsimile (it's so cheap that I refuse to give it free publicity, unless more than twenty people actually read this book). I live in Texas, so no liquor is available on Sundays. Since it was five in the morning, and I wasn't quite ready to start my day without breakfast, I popped open a Corona (yep, maybe not what you expected from the title, huh?) and searched, "why can't I buy liquor on Sundays in Texas?"

Turns out car dealerships and the liquor ban are laws left over from "blue laws." Apparently, these laws existed before Texas, or even the United States was founded. WTF?!? Ok, so I knew the liquor law had something to do with the religious beliefs of church. Drinking and driving is bad, but I guess drinking and praying is worse. As a kid, I remember attending mass, often next to some guy who reeked of alcohol, probably trying to remember what the hell he did the night before that he needed to repent for. I also remember my mom's boyfriend, a high school football coach, who stopped at convenience stores and made me, an eleven-year-old kid, buy him a six pack of beer he could drink while driving us back from some football conference in Albuquerque. Wow, how times have changed. As you read more, you'll notice that I go off on tangents pretty often. But too late, sucker, you already bought this shit. Err, at least I hope you did. Damn it!

In 321 CE (which I thought was BC, but if you don't know what I'm talking about look up CE), Emperor Constantine illegalized work on Sundays. Now, what does that have to do with liquor? Nothing, but the premise was set. Work was prohibited so people could attend church. Not getting it yet? Well, you're obviously not a drinker, or you haven't worked for anyone. Bro, people who can't drink after work have no reason not to tell their employers to fuck off. So, people are off on Sundays, and they think church is ok, but they think that wine is better. Consequently, people stopped working to get drunk and skip church. Yeah, real great idea Constantine. Eventually, the so-called leaders figured it out, and they banned liquor sales on Sunday. Then, hundreds of years later, dumbasses like me don't plan ahead and – voila – no liquor for my coffee.

Ahh, but I have a way around this. Not everyone in Texas has access to a military base, but I do. All I have to do is muddle through until 0900 (the equivalent of 9 a.m. for non-military people, or my veteran wife who forgot military time), and I can buy liquor on the base. It's still in Texas, but the Naval base decided *we do what we want* and didn't agree to the local liquor laws. God bless you, United States Navy.

I was in the Air Force, but I partied with some Navy SEALs more than once; they partied like they fought, and that's no joke. I partied with a lot of Navy folk in Panama (the country, not the city). As a matter of fact, four SEALs died to keep Panamanian leader Manuel Noriega from escaping on his private jet on December 20, 1989. I don't think too many people know that. Their names are Lt. JG John Patrick Connors, 25, Chief Engineman Donald Lewis McFaul, 32, Boatswain's Mate 1st Class Christopher Tilghman, 30, and Torpedoman's Mate 2nd Class "Ike" George Rodriguez III, 24. God rest their souls.

Since 0500, I have drunk a beer or three, researched blue laws, and started a book. Yep, that's how this shit got started. I ran out of the Bailey's facsimile. I'm sure that disappointment will be a consistent theme in this particular publication for some, especially those who are not veterans. Once again, you bought it buddy.

I'm currently semi-retired. I'll go into that more in another chapter. I still get up early, mostly, I have my coffee (from now on coffee with the Bailey's facsimile will hereby be known as "good coffee"), and I get my day going. I either exercise or help my wife with her business. The pay is terrible, but the benefits are amazing.

Being unemployed during the pandemic is a strange phenomenon. First of all, people are told that they don't have to look for work anymore. Then they started getting paid an extra amount. There has never been a better time to be unemployed in the history of the world.

As a semi-retired person, I have all kinds of free time, and yet my days fly by. Alcohol sales are up 55% – no shit! People work from home now, and production is up. You can't tell me weed and alcohol have nothing to do with that fact. And you have a bunch of unemployed people with nothing better to do than to watch Netflix (sales are also up) and drink. And smoke weed. I don't like weed personally, but I get it. And now the government is worried that people won't want to go back to work. No shit.

I have more time to reminisce. My wife, Carol, and I love to travel. I find myself fondly remembering cruises and trips to Mexico and the Dominican Republic. I even found myself planning to return to Panama after 30 years.

One of the things I remember the most about Panama is being drunk. Kind of an oxymoron, I suppose. Before the war, and after, Panama was a great place to party. There were an awful lot of Panamanians who really didn't like us, though, especially after the war. I speak Spanish, and I used the local bus system (because I was broke as hell while in the service). One time, it must have been around 0400, when I was returning from a night of drinking and dancing. I used the bus to get back to the base. We got close to the base, and I stood up and yelled "Para!" so the driver would stop while I made my way up to the front so I could get out. The driver slowed down, but he didn't stop. He rolled right by the base, and I told him to stop again. He smiled an evil grin and opened the bus door. It was clear he had no intention of stopping, which meant for me to jump out. I did and rolled down a muddy hill – it rained in Panama constantly. I walked up to the base gate. Two gate-guards belly-laughed at my muddy, bruised up dumb ass.

I also remember a lot of fighting, especially with Army guys. It was almost always over girls. The Army had some animosity toward the Air Force, and rightly so. Howard Air Force Base facilities were way better than Fort Kobbe (the Army). Crazy thing was, Kobbe was actually on Howard Air Force Base. Army guys would have to pass right by the plush Air Force barracks on their way to their run-down abodes. Despite the animosity, though, when it comes to fighting a common enemy, we're willing to die for each other.

I got in a fight at a nightclub called Patatus. A couple of guys decided that the guy I was hitting needed help and one attacked me from behind. A guy in the Army laid him out before he could do any damage. When the fighting was done, and we were all kicked out of the club (banned forever, they said, my ass), I thanked the guys who had stepped in.

One guy said, "Wasn't a fair fight. And besides, we're all Americans."

Chapter Two- Timing Is Everything

Pandemic Rule # 2- Always prepare for inclement weather before any excursion

One day people will be asking, "Where were you when the country shut down?"

Hawaii. Got one last vacation in before the shutdown was everywhere. I know, you sure as hell don't feel sorry for me. You're not meant to. I'm rubbing it in. After my next statement, though, you might actually feel a little sorry for me.

Carol and I have nine kids between the two of us. Nine! *Feel sorry for me now? No? You cold-hearted*...At the time of the shutdown, we had three grandkids and two on the way. We since have had two COVID-19 babies (born during COVID-19). Our son, Michael, is in the Navy. He and his wife, Lizze, were stationed in Japan, and we threw together a last-minute rendezvous in Hawaii. The plane tickets and stay were cheap. This was the beginning of March.

I'm not mentioning what airline we flew. It was great, and I totally would give them props, but the steward literally got me drunk. Free alcohol – the veteran's Holy Grail. It started with my favorite – coffee and *real* Baileys.

"Want a shot?"

"Of what?" I asked, doing my best to hide my enthusiasm.

"Whatever you like. How about tequila, cowboy?"

I had my hat and boots on. The steward liked me, maybe? Free alcohol, keep your eye on the ball Paxton.

"Yes sir, that works for me."

Several shots later, we landed in San Francisco. Good thing I wasn't driving. Both airports were not as busy as usual but still moving fairly normally. Masks and social distancing were not mandated yet. We ordered some pizza, I sobered up, and we hopped onto a plane to Hawaii. We had no complaints. I went into a pizza and tequila coma, and the next thing I remember, I awoke to the beautiful islands of Hawaii in the window.

I was born in Kauai. I hadn't been back to Hawaii since the seventies. It had been a dream of mine to return to my birthplace someday, but bad choices and life had gotten in the way. My wonderful wife had an awful lot to do with me finally making it back.

Now, I don't want to make anyone sick reading my little love story. I'll try to keep it to a minimum. I'm not bullshitting anyone in this book, though. If my wife was a bitch, I'd say so and live with the consequences. However, Carol is literally my best friend. We were bros long before we became hos. H-o-e-s? Not h-o-s-e. Well damn, you know what I mean. Carol is also a USAF veteran. She is patriotic and plays a mean game of pool. And darts. And softball. Yeah, she's a tomboy. And we have a great time doing absolutely whatever.

Any who, we arrived in Hawaii. We took an Uber to our Airbnb. The Airbnb people were like, "don't say anything to anyone about it being an Airbnb. Pick up your keys in the lockbox." It was all cloak and dagger because Hawaii taxes the hell out of everything, and they especially want their money on any place that's used in any way, shape or form like a hotel. Ho-tel. Ok, now I get it. It is h-o-s. Actually, it's h-o-e-s, but h-o-s makes better sense.

We met up with our kids and had an amazing dinner. I had more than a few coconut mojitos, which turned out to be the best mojitos I've had anywhere.

Fun on the beach. Fun at the Hawaiian strip clubs (not THAT much fun, you dirty-minded s.o.b.s). Great fish and Kalua pig, etc. It's Hawaii bro, nothing but a great time. Well, except for the part where we were stranded on a remote part of Kauai for a few days…

Even though I was born on Kauai, we decided on staying in Waikiki for economic reasons. I was born in Lihue and had never returned to my birthplace. It isn't like returning to your birthplace in Hobbs, New Mexico, or Lubbock, Texas. Hawaii is an awesome place to be from. I

mean, people are like, "where are you from?"
Paradise, bitch. So, we grab an island hopper
and head over to Kauai. That's me, my wife,
Michael, and his six-month pregnant wife, Lizze.
By the way, those two have a selfie game like no
one I've ever known. We swear they have some
hidden professional photographer who follows
them around all day. The only shitty pictures of
them are the ones I took.

Everything started off great. I had rented a Jeep,
but they had to upgrade me to a Jruck. You're
probably wondering what a Jruck is, right?
That's what I call their new Jeep truck, a Jruck. I
was stoked because I didn't think I would have
ever gotten to try a Jruck, rented or otherwise.
We drove to Wilcox Memorial, which was the
only thing left from my birthing way back at the
turn of the previous century. I took a shitty selfie,
but Michael and Lizze didn't bother because the
backdrop was a crappy hospital. It started to rain.

Next stop was Wailua Falls, a waterfall on the
island. The rain stopped, and we had just enough
time to take pictures like your typical tourists. A
lady was selling chocolate banana bread out of
her minivan, and it was amazing. I had already
decided we would drive along highway 56 to
Hā'ena State Park. We had an evening flight, and

it was not a terribly long drive. The rain had picked up again, so walking around a lot wasn't ideal. Anyone who's reading this right now and knows of Kauai is thinking "what a dumbass." Brah, I hadn't been back here since the 1970s. Give me a break.

Highway 56 snuggles right along the coast. The drive is beautiful: lush mountains on one side, and a beautiful ocean view on the other. So far, besides the rain, it was a great idea. We stopped at the last semblance of civilization in Hanalei. We got coffee at the Hanalei Bread Company. The coffee was great. The owner, I wish I remembered his name, told us we probably should get back before the water got too high and the Wainiha bridge would close. We had just passed the bridge, maybe fifteen minutes earlier, so we high-tailed it back and found a line of stopped cars.

Not two minutes after we had crossed over the bridge, the road workers decided to close it. Apparently, the water levels were on the brink until just then. So, we sat in the car line for a while. Carol walked out for intel. It was raining, but luckily my wife had suggested we buy ponchos at the local Walmart after we landed. Thank God.

Four hours they told her. Four hours and it would be back open. Probably. Well, we didn't come to Kauai to sit in a #$%^&! line of cars. We can do that back at home anytime. We drove back to Hanalei and had lunch at the local pub/grill. It was amazing, and the sun came out for a bit and we got double rainbow pictures. Carol and I looked like two old people in a blurry selfie: Michael and Lizze, movie stars. We got back on the road.

Just before arriving at the state park, the road had been washed out. There were surfboards, rolls of toilet paper, a few small boats, tires, and an assorted array of groceries and household items all over the place. Since I had a Jruck, I drove right through. Without a doubt, I can tell you I'm only alive because of the grace of God or luck or whatever you call it; it definitely wasn't for my brilliance. My wife thinks I'm bulletproof. Bullets have barely missed me. I've walked away from horrible car accidents, survived two falls over two stories high, and worked undercover narcotics for years. I'll probably die of something stupid, like a common cold or overeating. Or slipping in the shower.

We got to the state park and of course it was closed. The pandemic shutdown wasn't nearly what it would be in just a few days, but a lot of places were already closed. We turned around and drove back, stopping at a badass dry cave before reaching the Opakapaka Grill. We stopped there for – you guessed it – drinks. We killed a few hours there, but the constant pitter patter of rain killed my hopes of crossing back in time for our flight. We drove back to the now longer line, and Carol did more recon. The road workers told her we would be stuck here until midnight.

The local people of Kauai are awesome. They are the nicest people. Really, they have no excuse not to be nice– they live in paradise. Well, other than shit like this, which apparently happens pretty often. We drove back to the grill for dinner and drinks. The bartender was kind of cute, and with the drinks, she got cuter. I'm a flirt, and my wife knows it. She doesn't get wrung up about it either. We both notice the girl is flirting back for either a good tip (I said tip, ha ha) or she is just taking pity on an old man. Whatever, I'll take it. The owner said if we needed anything to just give him a call and gave Carol his number. Yeah, she gets flirted with a lot more than I do. I don't get wrung up about it, either. Flirtation at our age is just flattery.

We got back to the line way before midnight. If you ever want to test a relationship of any kind, just get stuck in a vehicle with them for an extended period of time. I can't bullshit you, though. We were all pretty cool; it could have been way worse. Someone came by and let us know a school opened up as a temporary shelter and the road would be closed until morning.

Because of Lizze's pregnancy, we opted to stay in the vehicle and not in the shelter. However, we did go to the shelter in the morning for free breakfast. Like I said, in general, Hawaiians are really nice people. Even the Haole, brah.

The following morning, I was cranky. It was still raining with no end in sight. We went to the store, and I bought a small grill and some big sausages. I was determined to make the most of this, even in my crankiness. We went to a park right next to the beach. Why a grill, wasn't it raining, you dumbass, you ask? One, I'm not brilliant, and two, I'm stubborn like no other. I have managed to grill in all sorts of terrains, from jungles to deserts. Once I even made snake stew for my squad during training in Nevada. Despite that rain, with some help from Carol we got the grill going under a tree, and we had some delicious sausages with Hawaiian bread. Much like hot chow tastes on the field, those dogs had that something extra that only those who have been there can understand.

Near the park, we noticed a copious number of cars parked, and yet, no one was around. I started thinking about why that would be. Someone was getting off this part of the island.

At this point, I'm feeling pretty desperate. My wife needed her meds, and Lizze was six months pregnant. We also had flights scheduled the next day. Highly motivated to get us off the island, I started calling helicopter and boat tour places and had no luck. Then, I stopped at the local surf shop so I could rent a boat. No boats. "But," the owner said, "you might be able to get a boat out at the pier. Yesterday, some guy was boating people across to Princeton." It was on.

We drove out to the pier, and sure enough, a few people were gathering. More parked cars, too. I did recon while everyone else packed our stuff up. Two Haole and a boat were running people back and forth as we spoke. We abandoned our Jruck and waited on the pier. We shared our ride with a super nice older couple from Michigan, and everyone was elated. It was like we were castaways finally getting saved. The boat ride was rough, yet the waters were still beautiful. The Haole got us close to the shore of an amazingly plush resort in Princeton. We were all a bit dirty, and we had to cross some rocks to the beach. The resort guests looked at us like we were illegal aliens crossing a watery border. Man, the situation was so Gilligan's Island. We made our way through a beautiful hotel resort and waited on an Uber. Somehow, despite the poor driver's car losing some piece of itself along the way and a tree down on a bridge, we made it to the airport and flew back to Honolulu. The rental car place was great; they had dealt with this type of situation before. The airline was cool, too. Our little adventure didn't end up costing us anything more than an extra day spent in a Jruck.

All four of us managed to change our flights around, get an extra day at our prospective hotels, and we all flew back. The airports in San Francisco and Dallas/Fort Worth were nearly empty, and so were the planes. The next day, the shutdown began. If anything had kept us from getting on a plane for just one more day, we would have been stuck in Hawaii. Any other time, it would have been totally acceptable, but in the times of COVID-19, Texas was definitely the better place to be. Timing is everything.

Chapter Three- Masks, Gas, and Ass

Pandemic Rule # 3- Always have proper cover in your possession

Oh yeah, it's about to get political up in here.

As I am writing this, masks seem to be a polarizing subject. Here we go. I'll lose "friends" and acquaintances after they read this book. Some will not get past this chapter. I've gotten into serious arguments with friends on Facebook (as many of you have), and still, I refuse to "unfriend" people because of their political beliefs. Even family relations are strained because we see things so differently.

I remember a time when people could disagree without losing their shit. I've had many arguments with friends and family, and it could go south pretty fast, but we always remained friends afterward. If you're reading this, and you decide to talk shit about the book, burn it, or unfriend me, bro – that's your American right. Unlike the United States, many countries don't allow opposing views. I joined the military to protect the country that affords us the rights to disagree and voice our opinions, even if that includes burning this book. Many people have chosen to turn around and shit on this country, disrespect the flag, and kneel for the anthem. As much as it infuriates me, that's their right, too. Let's get back to masks.

Masks and glasses don't work well together. They get fogged up, and then you've got to move shit around. I read that by wearing the glasses over the mask, they'll stop fogging up. Bullshit! And masks don't all fit the same even if that were true. Then, you have those who wear bandanas. If this was the year 1920, people would probably shoot you if you walked into a store with a bandana around your face. On a positive note, people with bad smiles have much more mask game. Halitosis? No problem, masks cover that shit up too. Masks are clearly not just for viruses anymore.

One thing the mask doesn't protect you from is a fart. During the pandemic, I've come across all sorts of flatulence that ripped right through the fibers in the mask. One day I was in a Walmart shitter and the guy next to me sounded like his insides were falling out of his ass. My mask did NOT protect me. If that mask can't stop a fart, I sure as hell can't figure out how it stops a virus.

After masks were mandated in Texas, coronavirus numbers increased. Is it because of the mask mandate? I don't believe so. I also don't believe a mask protects you from shit. I wear it where I'm asked to, but I would not wear it if I didn't have to. Does that mean I don't give a shit about others? Of course not. But some would have you believe that's true; if I wouldn't wear a mask without the mandate, then I'm some sort of asshole, at the very least, or a murderer, at worst. For years people have spread their shit around by going to work sick, coughing and sneezing without covering their faces, and not washing their hands. I get it – this virus is different. But, in so many ways, it's the same. I know a few people who have died from it, and I'm saddened they died. The reality is there are so many ways to die. A person could spend all of their time trying not to die, but they would still end up dying of old age, cancer, a heart attack, a meteor (could happen!), a car accident, a drone strike, a slip off the stairs or in the shower, spontaneous combustion, a drug overdose, starvation, suicide, homicide, suffocation, drowning, being eaten by pigs, a stray bullet, a remote-control plane gone haywire, overeating, overheating, or an STD you got before the pandemic. All people will inevitably meet their maker, be it COVID or otherwise, so why not enjoy your time on Earth to its fullest while you can?

Washing hands frequently and staying home when sick is what we should have been doing years ago. I've always hated sitting on a plane near sick people. I have no problem with requiring people with coughs and persistent sneezing to wear a mask because the spittle and mucous is just plain nasty. According to the World Health Organization, or WHO, there are nearly 650,000 deaths attributed to respiratory diseases linked to flu each year. At the time I'm writing this, there are 773,000 coronavirus-linked deaths in the world. I tried to find flu deaths for

2020, and even the WHO admits it's not known how many flu deaths were called coronavirus-linked deaths. I don't believe COVID-19 is not real. Hell, my wife and I had it. Strangely enough, we both got it after the mask mandate. That's not the point, though. COVID-19 has been seriously politicized by both parties. We watched doctors say masks were not helpful, then say they can help, then say they should be mandated. Other legitimate doctors and scientists disagree. Like the hydroxychloroquine issue. Some studies show if it's used early, then the death rates drop significantly. All it took was for 45th U.S. President Donald Trump to say it and people couldn't wait to debunk his statement, whether true or not. One last thing that scientists and doctors seem to disagree on: farts spreading the virus. Not even flatulence can escape COVID-19. Some studies suggest farts can spread the disease. They also say that covered asses are less likely to spread the virus, so in all fairness I guess that's a point in favor of masks. And pants.

You're probably sick of politics. So am I. I can't write about the pandemic without writing about politics. They go hand in hand.

Things don't make sense. I know there is someone somewhere with the exact opposite views as me writing something about the pandemic, too. He or she probably thinks people like me are blind or brainwashed, just like I think he or she is. Sadly, we may never be friends. Hey, I'm willing, but the other person probably isn't. We may have known each other in the past and had a beer together. Hell, we may have served together. The new intolerance for opposing beliefs divides us like nothing else in the USA has.

Chapter Four- Coronavirus, Cruises, and Casinos

Pandemic Rule # 4- Don't get stuck on a cruise with a bunch of sick people or you'll be on the longest cruise ever

Carol and I like to gamble. We haven't gotten to the point where we have to dig change out of the truck, borrow on our credit cards, or not be able to pay our bills. We definitely gambled a bit too much, though, this year. The shutdown actually was good for us, personally, in a lot of ways. We got a break from eating out and gambling. Our money actually stayed in our bank account for a while. But I'm getting ahead of myself.

In another chapter, I'll deal with the many, many benefits of old age. If you haven't figured out by now, I'm sarcastic (AF, as my children would write in a post or text message, and if you don't know what that means, you're more of a boomer than I am). I'm actually getting wayyyyy ahead of myself. Let's go back to a better time: a time when cruises and casinos were luring suckers like us onto their semi-luxurious boats and taking us to tourist-trap laden lands where suntan lotion costs thirty dollars.

In December of 2019, as the pandemic was barely a blip on the world's radar (thanks a lot WHO), we flew to Miami. I won a small jackpot at the local casino, and the next day, we boarded a Royal Caribbean cruise liner with the destination of Nassau, Bahamas. Little did we know this would be our last cruise for who knows how long. We had never bought the drink package before, but we decided to splurge.

Our four-day cruise began like many of my worst decisions in life did, with some strong drinks. It went from Mojitos to rum punch pretty quickly. My wife and I enjoyed the top deck with our ridiculously strong drinks. I stared at her smiling, glowing face, and her happiness made me happy.

Beauty is in the eye of the beholder. This is undoubtedly one of the most veracious statements ever written. The oldest recorded version of this statement is found in 3rd century Greece, and it has been restated hundreds of different ways since then. It's similar to "beauty is in the eye of the beer-holder," also a favorite saying of mine. Why did I bring this up? Because as I am staring at my wife's radiating smile, I see her beauty. But it reminds me of how people think of beauty so differently from one another, and the assumptions that they make because of that.

There was an incident a few years back that illustrates my point. I've had a lot of jobs in the past. As a narcotics agent, I worked regular jobs to appear more legit, sometimes full time. I've been a mover, a dishwasher, a pizza delivery man, a construction worker, a laborer at a secondhand store, and many, many sales jobs. After an early retirement, I went full-time into sales. One of my many positions was an online car-dealer of sorts, way ahead of its time. I delivered a Toyota 4Runner to a couple just twenty minutes from my home. I usually would Uber back to the office, but after about ten minutes of no Uber drivers picking up the ride, I called my wife. She was at the gym and would arrive shortly.

The better-half of the couple's ears perked up. "Hey, we can give you a ride. She doesn't have to leave the gym."

"She said she was done. It's no problem, really."

The lady smirked. "I bet she's some tall, hot California blonde." Her idea of beauty. Also, her assumption.

"She is from California, and she is definitely hot," I said, and smiled.

When my wife showed up, I texted her to come to the door. She texted back that she was sweaty and a hot mess. "Please," I texted. "Fine." I could read her frustration. But I couldn't help it.

My wife knocked on the door and the customer lady answered. Standing in front of the door was a short, voluptuous woman with an abundance of melanin. My idea of beauty.

"See, you were totally right about her being hot and from California."

My sense of humor is warped. Luckily, my wife loves me despite that. I'm a tall, big-boned cowboy type. Not a six-pack, actor-looking guy, but more of a retired linebacker look. My wife and I go to restaurants and sometimes people ask if we want separate checks. I think it's because she's black, not because she's short, and I'm usually wearing a straw cowboy hat and boots.

Why people would not think we're a couple is kind of a mystery to me. I'm pretty sure if I was black, even if I was in the same cowboy attire, people would assume we were a couple. Assume equals an ASS out of U not ME. I quit making assumptions years ago when I busted a Mennonite family hauling 60 pounds of cocaine. I know – MENNONITES! Tangents, here we are again.

My wife is beautiful. She has an amazing smile that literally lights up the room. Her energy is so amazing that she can have a roomful of rednecks scratching their heads saying, "you ain't like other black people." I'm not joking; I've seen it happen and have heard people use that very term. She breaks racial barriers and assumptions just by being herself. I'm going to delve way deeper into this racist shit later, but for now, back to the boat.

We spent the next day or so drinking and gambling. We danced one night. I'm a good dancer, not great, but good enough not to embarrass anyone. My wife is a great dancer. It took me months to learn how to Cumbia properly; it took her one night. The dance floor was covered with twenty-somethings. I was feeling very out of my element. They played some salsa, and we practically ran to the floor. There were a few other couples who could dance salsa, but we had people's attention (probably because we're that cute old couple). Later, they played some hip hop from the 2000s that I actually knew, and we danced to that. Suddenly, we were circled by twenty-somethings, and they were making a lot of hoopla over us. Cute old people dancing without looking like complete idiots? Or were we…

We arrived at a fake island in the morning. You might think I would be hungover, but I found all one needs to do to avoid the hangover is to stay drunk. Don't judge, readers! I wanted to get the most out of our drink package, and Carol wasn't keeping up. We trudged along the dock to the glorified water park that the cruise line calls "Perfect Day." There were some beautiful ladies dressed in traditional Brazilian Carnival-style attire. They were smiling and seemed genuinely happy. I got some pictures. Carol was worried about me because I had no suntan lotion. We approached a vendor, a woman in a small, wooden shack. In contrast to the pleasant dancers, this woman wore a seemingly permanent scowl. She barely answered us when we inquired about the cost of a four-ounce bottle. "Twenty-eight dollars." I'd rather burn. There is still a difference to me of being able to afford something and the principle.

"Perfect Day" was far from perfect. There was a costly water slide, a costly (and lame) zipline, and costly everything. It was an island that had been turned into a water park, and not even a good one. We hung out at the beach and had a few drinks. In all fairness to the creators of the fake island, we were a bit negative about it from the get-go, something that is definitely out of character for us. After a few hours, we returned to the boat. Someone needed a nap. Me.

When we left "Perfect Day," we were excited. Our next stop was Nassau, the reason we took this four-day trip. All napped up, I commenced to drink. Once again, Carol had tapped out, so I needed to drink her share, too. As we sailed off, the captain made an announcement. "Due to weather conditions, we will not be docking in Nassau." We were to have yet another day at sea, drinking and gambling. I was pissed, so I ordered a drink and headed to the casino. "I'll show them," I thought, as I gave the cruise my money. Strangely enough, I won a small jackpot, so I ordered a drink to celebrate. Liquor's amazing duality allows humans to drink out of happiness or sadness, and amplify any of the emotions within the positive or negative spectrum. The head of the casino told me I only needed a few more points to make it to some level where drinks would be free for a year, as well as upgrades, and honestly, he had me at free drinks because I can't say I heard anything else after that. But Carol heard, and we were to have free cruises all through 2020! Just in case you didn't get the irony, that was *free cruises all through 2020.*

Needless to say, we made whatever point level it was that we needed while giving back our winnings. And Florida's winnings. When we docked in Florida, I actually had drunk so much that I needed a break from drinking. I didn't think that was even possible. We called the cruise line's customer service to get some kind of refund or compensation for not going to Nassau. No one gets on a cruise with the sole destination being a glorified waterpark. They have a clause about not being able to control the weather. With all the weather tracking devices they have, and the years of experience on the sea, they could have made the trip to Nassau first. But that would not have been in the best interest of the fake island, which is owned by the cruise liner. God forbid customer satisfaction comes before the bottom line.

While this cruise was happening, Wuhan, China, was in the middle of a coronavirus outbreak. It was barely a blip on the radar. Later we found out about cruise ships that hadn't been allowed to dock for weeks on end.

Chapter Five- Staying Alive

Pandemic Rule # 5- Keep your friends close (socially distanced, of course), but keep your sanitizing supplies closer

The Great American Lockdown meant different things to different people. For most Americans and small businesses, it meant a time of fear, loneliness, and economic hardship. For places like Walmart and Amazon, it meant business as usual. Despite the stock market crash, which also crushed many people's 401Ks, certain businesses saw their shares rise exponentially later. There I go getting ahead of myself yet again.

At the time of the lockdown, we were told masks didn't help and to shelter in place. But you can go to the grocery store. Certain workers were deemed "essential," but everyone else was ass-out. I already didn't have a job. I never told you about that, did I? I'll give you the quick rundown.

In 2019, I started working for a home builder in sales. I had a solid record in every sales job I've ever had, and they hired me to work in an area that was known to be somewhat slow in sales. I worked every day up to our "grand opening" and consequently outsold everyone. I was also driving roughly three hours a day. I know there are people with longer commutes. My arms were in pain from the driving. I had lost a lot of mobility in them over the last decade, and the VA doctors finally determined after painful physical rehab and numerous drugs that both of my elbows have severe osteoarthritis. It was not going to get better, and the excessive driving didn't help. The company I worked for had numerous other neighborhoods, some much closer to where I lived. I was the number-one guy in my area, so I thought they could move me somewhere closer.

"You know, there are people who endure a lot more to get to an amazing job." The regional manager went into a story about some physically disabled person, and her story, and went on and on, basically telling me I was a pussy. Here's the thing- it wasn't that I *couldn't* bear the pain and discomfort. *Suck it up, buttercup.* The fact is, no matter how amazing the position was, I didn't *have to* bear shit. She gave me some crap about if I stayed a little longer, she'd find an opening somewhere closer. That story went on for a few months. I knew she wanted me to finish the year in that neighborhood, and I knew I was being handled, so I gave my medical letter that I had shown to her to the human resources department who then put me on medical leave. After months of waiting for the VA to give me an appointment for a specialist, the home builder decided to let me go. I wasn't upset. I wasn't happy with the way they dealt with me, and they weren't happy with me forcing the issue. Crazy thing is, though, if they had just moved me somewhere closer to my house, I'd probably still be there, and I guarantee I'd be the number one person there, like I was when I left.

Don't get me wrong – I'm grateful for the opportunity. Sometimes there just isn't a good fit between an employee and an employer, and I've got no hard feelings. Back to the lockdown rant.

Now, I'm unemployed during the lockdown. We have been told masks are bad. Shelter in place. Stay home. Walmart is okay. Church is bad. Movies are okay now, but they weren't. Casinos were bad, but now, they too, are safe. Walmart and other grocery stores are okay. Just distance yourself. The fact that we could still go to Walmart and other grocery stores but not to small businesses or churches or any kind of restaurant, well, I knew it didn't make sense. I use the Walmart example because almost everyone goes to Walmart. It was the same for all the convenience stores and supermarkets. And the liquor stores. Amen to that one, but come on, if you can go to all these places, then you can go to an outdoor church at the very least.

I know I've mentioned church a lot. I am not a big church goer. But I absolutely believe people should always have that outlet. I believe one hundred percent in our constitution. And if anyone with any sense at all studies it, learns the back and forth between opposing sides while the forefathers were creating it, and understands that the same concerns the forefathers had are the same concerns we have now, well, let's just say you'd get it too. I really think that people believe that just because something was created several hundred years ago it isn't relevant; that the people back then were less sophisticated or intelligent. The reality is that we are just as smart, or not, and just a sophisticated, or not, as we were hundreds of years ago. In fact, our forefathers were avid readers and inventors, and most of us in today's world are not. What really separates us from our ancestors is technology.

We spent the next month or so saving money. We organized a thank you lunch and a thank you dinner for all of the workers at a local hospital. We just wanted to do something positive. After seeing so much negative bullshit on social media, we decided it would be good to promote something positive, so we asked for donations and videoed the lunch and dinner. Sadly, there were some people who still found negative things to say, even about this. Strangely enough, none of my friends who kept posting negative, anti-president, anti-freedom comments and memes donated to our meals for healthcare workers. Even the ones who posted memes about thanking healthcare workers. Not one.

For a while I kept finding myself getting into unwinnable arguments with ex-coworkers and classmates. I even took the time to present my adversaries with evidence supporting my position or claim, sometimes from the very places they themselves sometimes cited. It seemed like they were unable to read what was right in front of them; it was as if they had some sort of logic dyslexia. Realizing that no matter how logical or fact-based my arguments were, these friends would not even try to see something that didn't fit in their new belief system.

A few good things did come about on social media. I'm a New Mexico Military Institute alumnus. A very attractive classmate from Albuquerque organized a Thursday virtual happy hour. Right up my alley. Not in a sexual way. In a drinking way. You people really have dirty minds, you know?

We Zoomed together week after week. Some of my fellow alumni had taken the happy hour very seriously and would go on some drunken rants. It was hilarious. And therapeutic. We connected with people that we hadn't seen in years and made new friends as well.

Carol immersed herself in learning via YouTube. Have I mentioned that my wife is brilliant?

Chapter Six- The Great Debate

Pandemic Rule # 6- Always avoid talking about religion and politics to your friends and neighbors-especially if you like your car's paint job

"I have a prediction, boo, that this debate will be a huge shitshow." I swear by all the beers and booze in the world that it's exactly what I told my wife the day of the first debate between Trump and Joe Biden. I imagined the movie, Grumpy Old Men, with Jack Lemmon as Biden and Walter Matthau as Trump, and of course, the new hot neighbor would be the U.S.A. Man, was I right.

I really don't give a shit who you voted for. Truly, I don't. I firmly believe in the Constitution and that all Americans have the right to vote for whoever the shit they want to. I also believe the country is better balanced with opposing viewpoints. I don't believe that I should cancel you, or you me, simply because we don't agree. That rhymes, don't you see? After looking up a hundred or so quotes by smarter people than myself on debate, I decided to quote myself instead. Healthy debate is the mother of peaceful compromise and thereby change. Feel free to quote me. It's badass.

I support Trump. Well, now half of my readers who may have still been with me up to this point just tossed the book in the trash. But that's what I'm talking about. Everyone believes they're right, but worse yet, they believe that those who don't agree with them are just plain evil. Few people think, "Well, I know I'm wrong, but the hell with it. I'll continue to –." Shit, actually, yes, they do. You know what I mean, though. Catholics and Christians believe Jesus is the only way, while the followers of Islam believe Muhammad is. They've been at each other's throats for more than a thousand years. Now, democrats and republicans are doing the same thing. But what makes you more correct than me? Or me than you?

Despite my support of Trump, I didn't think highly of his performance in the first debate. Nor did I care for Biden's. And frankly, Chris Wallace did his best on handling those two, but I think he could have done a better job on some of his questions for both men. He had a chance to ask questions that could have really defined the debate, and he did some, but there were more questions that were just mainstream-media appeasing. Who knows, though, maybe even had Chris Wallace asked a few questions that were more related to policy and less to his unpopularity, Trump may still have gotten off-course and Biden may still have evaded them. And Wallace DID bail Biden out more than once.

I turned on CNN for a bit. Their polls had Biden winning by roughly 60 percent. I turned on Fox. They had Trump winning by roughly 60 percent. I shook my head and laughed. Did anyone see the debate Carol and I saw? Carol and I agreed the real loser of the debate was America.

I read posts from my Trump-supporting acquaintances and friends talk about how Trump really showed Biden. I saw others posting about how Biden "showed restraint despite Trump's bullying" and he did well despite Trump talking over him. I disagree with their outlooks. Biden used unfounded information immediately in the start against Trump, both about the tax return and the supposed "losers" statement. Trump used Hunter Biden's drug addiction. Meanwhile, everyone was distracted by the grumpy old men routine and didn't notice when Biden evaded some key questions and Trump missed great opportunities to talk about what he had done and wanted to do. Biden had a few good hits: the best when he addressed his son's drug addiction. All in all, this debate could have been from the Geraldo Rivera show back in the day. A few flying folding chairs would have made for a great ending and a better overall debate.

By the way, I'm not trying to change anyone's mind here. That isn't the purpose of this book. By the time the book is on the market, the election will be over. Not sure if we'll know who the winner is though.

My Beautiful Bella

I'm dedicating a part of this chapter to my dog, Bella. The year 2020 was crazy from the beginning to the end. The night before writing this chapter, the dog police took my Bella away for attempted murder. Or maybe murder, I'm not sure of the other dog's status yet. Some people reading this will take it the wrong way. I don't take what happened lightly. I take all tragedy lightly because if you can't have a sense of humor about the shit that happens in life, then you'll be a grumpy old fuck before your time.

I met Bella three years ago at the local shelter. I opted to adopt a dog. As soon as I saw her, and she saw me, I knew she was my dog, and I was her dad. A black and white, pit-terrier mix, she stood regally and wagged her tail at me as I approached the cage. Carol wanted to see other dogs, and we did, but for me, there was no other.

I have a little touch of PTSD. Bella calmed me down. She kept me company when my wife was out of town. She made it easier for me in rough and sometimes lonely moments. She was sweet and was loved by all the family. But, like her dad (me), she had some issues. If you've never heard of leash aggression, that makes two of us. When she was on a leash and saw other dogs, she wanted to attack them. She went from this sweet, loveable being to a killer in mere seconds. It made it really hard to take her for walks, and we had a few problems when she got out of the yard.

We hired a German dog-trainer to help out. This was shortly before the pandemic. When the lockdown happened, training was cut short, and the lady refunded us. I really think she just saw Bella as too hard and quit, but maybe she was just being nice because of the situation. Either way, last night Bella got out of the fence because of a defective door that was installed. She attacked a dog and bit a person who intervened (he is okay). Because of the other incidents, and the fact that my neighbors were now terrified of her, I gave custody to the animal control officer. He told me she would probably be retrained, not euthanized, and I admit that while that was a relief, I sorely miss my crazy, sweet, pretty companion. This was strangely one of the hardest things I've ever been compelled to do, and it'll hurt for a long time.

Chapter Seven- Finances and Fuckery

Pandemic Rule # 7- Always take advantage of a good crisis

Ignorance is bliss, and it will also keep you poor.
I quit writing for a few months. I do that. I write
like a madman for a few weeks and then put it
away. I get busy doing life stuff. I don't know. I
told you, I'm not super religious, but I had a chat
with God this morning. It was a bit one-sided, or
so it seemed. When I wrote my first two books,
Cartel Rising and The Plaza, I wished to be a
full-time writer. I fantasized about it. I worked as
a contract undercover agent, or UC. It sounds
pretty cool, right? It isn't that cool. I'd say most
of my time as an agent, the government funded
(your tax dollars and government seizures at
work) me to drink, pay for strippers, and get
reasonably good at pool. That is another story
that I may or may not write for another book. Ah
crap, the tangent police just showed up.

I "retired" in 2010 from my contract work. I went
full time into my other job – sales. I've been
writing for years now. I wrote Cartel Rising over
a ten-year period. I wrote The Plaza in one year. I
took a year off in 2012, and I wrote Lily Without.
I was broke as hell during that year, but I loved
doing nothing but exercising and writing. I was
in amazing shape, too. I went back to work (I
wasn't very good with money before, which I'll
discuss later) and fell into a terrible depression. I
bought lottery tickets, so I could win and just

write. Silly, and a common fantasy, I'm sure, but I was desperate. As I said, I'm currently unemployed. I've assisted my wife with our family business, and we've made some good investments. So I now have time to write every day if I want. And that was part of what my conversation with God was about.

First, I let God know that I was so very grateful for this amazing life. We have great kids, I have a great wife, and opportunities abound, even during the pandemic. And I realized I was in the position that I had always wanted to be in so many years ago. All I had to do was start taking advantage of it. I told God that I would. And I thanked God once again. Being grateful is an important part of life, religious or not. I prayed when I was in law enforcement, a whole lot of times, but mainly because I was in some serious shit at the time, but I can't say I was particularly grateful. Gratitude can literally change your life. Perception is your reality. If you're grateful for what you have, and you don't focus on what you don't have, your mindset has changed and your life will be better, despite there being no actual physical changes to it. Look, I'm not saying that you shouldn't want more out of life, just the contrary, but be grateful for all that you have no matter what stage of the game you're at.

After realizing just exactly where I was actually at in life, I made a commitment. I'm currently living my dream. No lottery wins, yet we're able to comfortably live and I can still write nearly full time, even if it may only be for a year or two. If you're reading this and thinking, "well good for you," dude, don't be a dick. I have a point here. Opportunities are often right in our faces and we refuse to recognize them because they didn't present themselves to us the way that we had imagined them. Sometimes God doesn't hold the door wide open so we can saunter on through. Instead, he will crack a window that we have to open all the way up by ourselves, maybe even have to go over some broken glass, to end up where we had prayed we would.

On to finances – I spent freely, nearly all of my life. Had I read *Rich Dad, Poor Dad*, I may have changed that behavior. I was a late bloomer in that aspect. Once I understood the importance of investments, and the fact that one can make money without a job in any economy (entrepreneurship), my eyes were opened. Our country is amazing. Our history, like the history of mankind, is not pretty. Growth hurts. Evolution is not an easy nor pretty process. And no human-made process is perfect, period. But wow, there's so many amazing stories we rarely hear about. And this is where I believe the fuckery begins.

The first female American self-made millionaire was Madam C. J. Walker. I'm surprised if you haven't heard of her. Her story finally went mainstream. Want to read some amazing stories of black entrepreneurs you probably haven't heard of? Just look up Frank McWorter, Robert Gordon, James Forten, and William Alexander Leidesdorff, Jr., to mention a few. When I went to school, not only was I not taught about black entrepreneurs, but I was also not taught about entrepreneurship in general. Nor the thousands of success stories of Americans who have changed their lives, their communities, their nation, and some, even the world with their inventiveness and entrepreneurship. Sadly, my only real classes in finances were how to work hard and save money. Even my grandfather, who was amazingly adept at his finances, never taught me anything about investing. Ignorance is not bliss. Ignorance is an excuse to be lazy.
If you're struggling financially and are sick of it, reach out to me. I'll include an email for anyone to reach out. I'm sure I'll get some amazing emails about how I suck and my book is trash or I should go to hell because I supported Trump and all that, but for those of you who truly want

some answers, I will send them to you. For free. All I ask in return is that once you have it figured out that you teach someone else. Your children. A friend. Your mom. It doesn't matter. Let's not continue the fuckery and hide good financial sense from others. What is this fuckery you speak of?

For some reason, a small portion of society believes that only they should have the key to success. The knowledge they pass on from generation to generation is kept secret from mainstream society. Highly successful Native Americans like Maria Tallchief, Jim Thorpe, James McDonald, and Susan La Flesche Picotte are not spoken of in school. Americans like Robert S. Abbott, Richard Allen, and Ella Baker, who are also highly influential, are not taught about. Not all of these people were financially successful, either. But all of these people were successful in their own rights, and they have proven over and over that there is no suppression or system stronger than what the human mind can accomplish. These are the things that should be taught in school, rather than how awful our history is or how some are very lucky and others are not.

Speaking of native Americans, how about them Cleveland Indians? They're going to change the name. I'm wondering who has the name actually been offending other than the woke? Their name was in fact started by the fans of the then Cleveland Spiders, named for the first Native American in the majors, Louis Sockalexis. I don't see how changing the name honors him in any way. I'm sure that he was probably mistreated by many of his contemporaries, and who knows how many racial slurs were thrown at him by ignorant, racist fans, but I fail to see how changing the name will restore Louis's honor or name by giving people one more way to forget the past. Or his accomplishments.

The fuckery of the world is the propagation of the idea that YOU are not in control of your life. You *are* absolutely in control. And the outcome you create is not always the outcome you seek. The creation of a specific, positive outcome is the product of vision, perseverance, and consistency. Your skin color, your accent, or your height do not create the outcome that you wish to create, nor does anyone else truly hold power over you or your dreams. You and you alone must decide what your success will be. Enough of that. Votes are still being recounted, and it does appear there was some fuckery involved. I suspect we shall see later that there was a lot more than people want to admit. If you're okay with any amount of voter fraud, regardless of its outcome, there's something wrong with your reasoning. I totally get that there are so-called "acceptable" amounts, and that verifying every vote is virtually impossible, but I see no issues with enforcing voter laws that limit voter fraud without being an undue hinderance for voters. I've lived in Mexico and stayed in many South American countries and have seen first-hand the consequences when people allow fraudulent voting to occur. And yes, it's the people. We allow those in power to be in power. Please don't forget that.

Chapter Eight- Couldn't Find a Can in Cancun, or the Cancun Cops Caper

Pandemic Rule # 8 - Look for airline specials on off-seasons
            and #9- Plan ahead for trips, and for *bathrooms*

Carol and I love to travel. I really think it's one of the reasons we both like gambling. That said, we quit gambling a few months ago. Not forever, just a good, much-needed break. But we needed somewhere to go. We searched online and decided to head to a place that had eased up on their restrictions – Cancun. We'll be undoubtedly ostracized by all those who believe staying at home will stop the virus. Those same people make trips to the store to buy groceries and liquor, and probably buy gas, too. How they think they're somehow safer than us is a mystery to me. No one is safe. Life is not safe.

We flew to Cancun a few weeks before the election. The flight was cheap, and we secured an all-inclusive resort at a highly discounted price – all we had to do was go to their timeshare presentation. We've done them before. I secured us a rental car. I worked and lived in Mexico for twelve years (five during the drug war in Mexico between El Chapo and all the other cartels), so driving around there is not an issue. We love to have our freedom and go where we want when we want and how we want. Our saying is, "we do what we want!"

The city had just been through a hurricane. It was a risky move, but we figured God would spare Cancun another hurricane for at least a week or so. We arrived at the airport, and the guy who I had arranged to rent a car from was waiting for us. We drove to our resort and checked in. There is a machine that mists you whenever you enter the resort. I'm assuming it's supposed to kill the virus without killing the host. At least that's what I hoped.

Shortly after checking in, we promptly acquired two, excellent double piña coladas and we enjoyed them out on the beach. The weather was warm and partly cloudy, perfect for beach walks and drinks. We had a few more drinks, ate dinner, and returned to the beach with yet more drinks. The water was amazing; we swam a little. Upon returning to the hotel lobby, our ears perked up to the sounds of salsa (the music, not the edible kind), and we found ourselves dancing and drinking. It felt like normalcy. After a while, our age caught up with us, and we returned to our room and slept like babies.

The next day was our "presentation." It was great. They liquored us up. They took us on a boat ride. It's strange how all these timeshare places like to say they aren't timeshares. Wherever you go, they're always somehow "unique" and not really a timeshare, yet the sales pitch and the sharing of time in the resort are always the same. They hit us up for 140,000 dollars, I shit you not. By the end, it was down to 5,000, and we still walked.

That night, we decided to check out the nightlife. Strip clubs tried their best to lure us in, and the night clubs all had people waiting to get in due to limited capacity. We opted for tacos and a few beers and decided to press on. I couldn't find a bathroom anywhere on the way to our car, so I handed the car keys to Carol, stopped behind a truck in a seemingly desolate parking lot, and peed. As I zipped up, I saw three Cancun cops running to cut me off. I spoke to them in Spanish and raised my arms to let them know I was neither a dangerous criminal nor trying to escape. Two female officers and a male officer surrounded me. They were all much shorter than me. I thought of three regular size cops surrounding Hulk Hogan.

"Sir, you were seen relieving yourself in public."

"Yes, I couldn't find a bathroom fast enough and needed to pee."

"You can't just pee wherever you like."

"I understand that, so I peed discreetly behind a truck."

"Not so discreetly, sir. We saw you."

"Yes, because you were looking for it, which is understandable. That's your job."

"We weren't looking for anything – my partner here clearly saw you. Have you been drinking?"

"I had a couple of beers with my tacos earlier. I'm a disabled veteran, and I have a prostate condition. I can't hold it for long, and we tried to get into that club over there, so I could pee and they wouldn't let me."

"Well, sir, a medical condition doesn't give you the right to pee wherever you like. You should take that into consideration. Especially when you have been drinking. You know you have a condition, so you shouldn't be drinking at all. Now, we're going to have to take you in to see the judge. He'll impose a fine, and if you don't pay, then you'll be in jail for thirty-six hours."

I lived and worked in Mexico for 12 years. I've been traveling to Mexico and South America for more than a lifetime. I understood what kind of a game this was. If these cops wanted to arrest me, they would have already done so. The male officer got tired of the game and took his leave.

He was older, and I'm pretty sure he recognized that I wasn't going to be intimidated into giving them money. Carol walked up to us, appearing much more upset than she really was.

I said, "Hey, I understand the situation. You guys can do what you need to."

"What's going on?" Carol asked, her anguish readily expressed in her eyes and lips.

One of the officers spoke to Carol in broken but very understandable English. I was impressed. She explained the need for arresting me, the judge, and harped upon the thirty-six hours.

"What? No! My husband has a medical condition!" Carol started to cry. I nearly laughed. You have to understand, my wife is not a crier. She's tough. She's a veteran!

As if on cue, I put my hands in front of me and told the officers they would have to cuff me in front because my elbows are jacked-up and my arms won't go behind my back, all true. The cops spoke in police code for a second. The cop who spoke broken English explained we could pay them the fine and be done with it. Carol looked at me, and I knew she was thinking of bargaining, but these cops had spent too much time not arresting me, and I was wearing them down. I said "no way" to her with my eyes and she understood.

"Officers, I'm sure the judge will not penalize me when we go in front of them. I have proof of my medical condition. And if I have to pay a fine, then so be it. I really don't mind taking a chance with the legal system here in Mexico. I'm sure that it is a fine system indeed."

The two cops looked like they wanted to laugh, or cry, I'm not sure which. Exasperated, they talked to each other again. They turned to me and Carol. "We're going to let you go, this time."

"Oh, thank you!" Carol genuinely looked *relieved* (yes, a pun, because I was the one that was really relieved). One cop went on to lecture me again and told me they were letting me go because of my wife, and I need to be more responsible, blah blah blah. Like a child who had just been lectured, I nodded emphatically, yes mom, I understand, and the cops finally left.

Chapter Nine- Uncle Tom

Pandemic Rule # 10- You might get another chance to attend a person's wedding, but you won't get another chance to attend their funeral

There you go thinking negatively again. My uncle was named Tom Powers. We just attended his funeral. He passed after having dementia the last several years of his life. I've never been one to put a dead person on a pedestal just because he's dead. And I'm not putting Tom on one, either. But his life, and death, affected many people in a way that impressed upon me how one person can truly influence a great many others, without Facebook, without the internet, without an ounce of fame or a ton of money.

Being brutally honest on paper is the easy part. Knowing people will read this, people who know you, that's the hard part. I refuse to be hypocritical and mince words or hide details because of that. You'll understand why I prefaced this chapter like this later.

I didn't know Tom Powers that well. I hardly know most of my blood-relations. One of the greatest family-related influences I can remember was actually when I lived with another family for a time in Roswell, New Mexico.

Another tangent-moment!

My mother had some serious substance abuse issues and psychological issues. I left home more than once. The last time I left I was fifteen. I had only returned to live with her after having spent the last few years living "abroad." For some reason, I can't recall if I lived with the Gibbs family before or after this incident.

Memories are strange things. I've blocked that shit out, which I'm sure wasn't that great in the first place so some of this isn't all that clear. I remember I had an amazing friend, Sgynman Gibbs, who somehow hoodwinked his mom and dad, Esther and William Gibbs, to let me live with them. Sgynman and his sister, Kelly, became my brother and sister. And I became their lightest-skinned sibling.

I don't remember race ever being an issue, or even a theme. I wore Sgynman's dew cap to bed one night. It did make my hair a bit wavy, but the way Sgynman laughed about it was the best. I loved the blue Kool-Aid and the cornbread with buttermilk, and the warm nights playing hide-and-seek. Sgynman always found me because he said I was the only one who glowed under the moon. We shared a bed! No one is that gracious, but I'll be damned if he wasn't. When his cousin,

Stephen, came over, we would all stay in that bed. I can to this day recall the sound of the fan and smell of feet. Oh, and Stephen had a bad-ass Audi we sometimes cruised in, "Posse on Broadway" bumpin'.

Mr. Gibbs was in the Korean war. He limped because of a bad case of the gout. He was a stern man with a good heart, and he was a preacher. Mrs. Gibbs was, and still is, an amazing singer. I have no doubt that she loved, and still loves me, like one of her own. In all fairness, she is the only real mom I ever have known. Kelly was my little sister who quietly schemed in her own room. I say schemed because behind that shy, quiet façade was a smart and wonderful woman-to-be. She was always accepting and loving, and I'll never forget that. I'm not going to go into a ton more of details because that would be another book itself.

I mention them because they had a powerful and positive influence over me. I failed them because I let things distance us. I love them and will never forget the brief but precious time I had as a part of their family. I hope they know how deeply I regret not staying a part of their lives more.

Anyway, I was estranged from my family at an early age and literally had no contact with my father or anyone on his side of the family until I was around nineteen. I was on leave after a temporary duty, or TDY, and my now ex-wife had a friend who she wanted to visit in Levelland, Texas. We drove there and visited, and on the way out, I noticed a billboard saying "Paxton Real Estate." Knowing I had a lot of Paxton family in Texas, I decided to swing by their office and see if we were related.

I told my story to a man named Eddie Paxton.

Eddie looked shocked. "Son, I don't believe this. Your father is my brother. I know he had been looking for you. I just can't believe that you're here, in my office."

I hadn't seen my father since I was eight years old. Uncle Eddie called my father, and we were connected. Eddie was in tears.

Fast forward many years later. A pandemic has shut down the entire country. Trump is president, and everyone has to wear masks in public. I've been very busy in my life and have lived all over the world. My father calls to tell me that he and his wife, my bonus mom, Tammy, are on the way to Houston because uncle Tom is in bad shape. Oh, and by the way, they had a terrible accident a few days earlier while driving from Delaware to

Texas that totaled their car. But they're okay. Shaking my head.

A few days later, Tom passed, and we planned to head out to the funeral. My aunt Yvonne (Tom's wife, my dad's sister) really wanted me and Carol to go. We were honored. I learned so much during that short trip.

For those of you thinking, "Oh my God, going to a funeral during COVID-19, what's wrong with you people?", this is Texas. If you drive to any small town here and stop in any old gas station, you'll see young and old alike not wearing masks and not changing the way they live because of a virus. It's the way of the Texans. Out here, many of us believe that personal health and safety is just that –personal. Everyone has the right to stay home, wear a mask, etc. We also have the right to live normally and not in fear. Back to Tom and Yvonne.

Their love story is movie worthy. Some of this I knew from my father. Some of this I learned at the service. The pastor was brilliant, by the way. I truly hope I'm not messing this up because Tom was a fine man, and my aunt Yvonne is an amazing lady. They met sometime in the early 1960s at a mortgage company where they both worked. Yvonne was married at the time, and Tom was recently separated from the Air Force. No! There you go thinking dirty again. It wasn't like that. They were work friends. Yvonne's husband at the time was a race car driver. Her husband had a horrible accident, right in front of her and the kids.

I don't believe for a second that Tom swooped up Yvonne in her moment of need. Did he probably already fancy her? Of course, he did. He was human. My aunt was, and still is, a good-looking woman with a kind heart. But Tom was a man of principles, and I assure you that while Yvonne was married, he would not have acted upon any ill intentions. What he did do, though, was offer her and the kids his love and support. And they fell in love.

My father had told me that Tom was the man who showed him how to truly be a man. Not the John Wayne bravado bullshit that he and later I learned from the street and the movies, but the kind of man who is consistent, loving, and thoughtful. Not this pussy, connected-to-your-emotions bullshit kind of guy, but simply a man of his word. A man who believed in Christian principles and actually followed them. A man who put God and family first all of the time. A man who loved another man's children as much as he did his own.

It was the 1960's, and my dad was a newly enlisted sailor in the Navy. When he had returned from the China seas, he learned of the death of his former brother-in-law. Tom wanted to speak to him.

Tom said, "Guinn, I want you to understand something. I know you're basically the man of the house. I love your sister, and I love her kids. I'll take care of them and protect them with my life."

This was not something that just any man did back then, or would do now, for that matter. Tom wanted to make sure my dad knew his intentions with his sister and the kids were true. He certainly didn't have to do it. My dad may have been skeptical, but he was certainly impressed. While a caring man, Tom wasn't a pushover. Not even a little. A few years later, while my dad was on leave, Tom called him. All he told him was that he needed him. By now, he had more than earned the respect of my father.
When my dad arrived to Houston, the two headed for Dallas. "Guinn, my sister needs me. She's afraid her asshole husband is going to beat her, again. We should get there before he gets home from work, but I need you to go with me because I'm afraid if I see him, well, I might just kill him. I want you to keep me from doing that.

71

Killing another man like that, well, it just ain't right."

I watched the many pictures of Tom on the wall of the church behind the pulpit. Military, bike races, fishing, cruises. As the pastor started to speak about Tom being a good, Christian man, and I believe he definitely was, pictures of Tom at a luau popped up. He was wearing a Hawaiian grass skirt and coconut bra, dancing with some pretty hot dancers. I laughed, albeit quietly, recognizing the inopportune moment for those images to appear.

My bonus mother read a letter that Tom had left in his workshop for his family. He had obviously known that he had dementia but had still been lucid when he wrote the letter. Tom addressed his most cherished family, his wife and children. He told them how proud he was and how lucky he had been, among other more personal things. I like to think of myself as a writer, but Tom's simple, yet eloquent letter far surpassed anything I have ever written. In its powerful and meaningful prose, he was able to convey the lifetime of love that he felt for his family in such a way that no one in the church that day would ever forget. To simply say that the letter was moving would be doing it an injustice.

My cousin sitting in front of me broke down a bit. Feeling his anguish, I squeezed his shoulder and was glad I was there for him.

The pastor did a great job. He did not know Tom, but he had learned a lot about him by speaking with family and friends. One of the points he made in the sermon was that Tom was still doing good works by bringing us all together even in his passing. Tom had done just that by re-connecting a family that hadn't seen each other in thirty years. I was grateful because now I was finally ready to connect with them as well. Having been estranged from my family at an early age, I grew up basically alone. By the time I found my father, I had already gone a very different direction. As time passed, I struggled with my relationship with my father and bonus mom, and my sisters. Thinking I was basically the black sheep of the family, I never felt comfortable around them. Over the last six years, I have made changes in my life that have been instrumental in my happiness.

Happiness is defined in as many ways as there are IPAs in Portland or corrupt politicians. You get the point. I believe wholeheartedly that any true happiness one can find actually comes initially from within. Perhaps you, the reader, have known that. I didn't. I thought happiness was family, money, success, alcohol, sex, etc. If you aren't happy with yourself, you're never really happy. Obvious when stated, but easier said than done. I believe that Tom was a happy man because he was comfortable with himself, first, and the rest of his life was a consequence of that. Driving back from Houston, Carol told me something I wasn't expecting.

"I've never seen you so at ease with people."

"Not even with your family? C'mon." I get along famously with Carol's amazing family.

"No, seriously. Never."

I thought about why that may be, and the answer suddenly seemed clear. "Before I was never successful enough, in a bad relationship, hell, I felt I was too fat. It kept me from attending school reunions, family reunions, you name it. For the first time in my life, I'm comfortable with myself."

If I could influence half as many people as my uncle Tom did, and the way that he did, I would be a very happy man.

Chapter Ten- Trump, Tomfoolery, and a Tampered Election?

Pandemic Rule # 10- Avoid joining any mobs, period

Many will read this and say that Carol and I bought into Trump's hype, that we're part of a cult, etc. I'm not going to waste time trying to convince anyone they're wrong or that their entire belief system is corrupt. No one believes the truth until it smashes them in the face.
I believe in facts and not in coincidences. A "tampered" election doesn't have to be all fake votes, either. The fact is that several swing state's election processes were changed without the state's legislature being the ones to make those changes, all prior to the 2020 election. Those changes resulted in numerous unverified votes being counted: votes that under normal conditions would not have been counted. Both social media and the mainstream media were literally stacked against the president from the get-go of his election, more so than any other time in America. The fact that in this election, during the pandemic, with a lackluster leader barely in charge of the DNC, without rallies and

a low viewer turnout for all his virtual rallies and speeches, Biden somehow pulled off the most votes for any president of the U.S., ever, also lends credence to a tampered election. I do not, and will not, believe that the DNC did anything but pull off the biggest heist in United States history. They wanted Trump out, and they were willing to do it by any means necessary.

I watched the United States royalty known as the Senate and the House cringe in fear as a crazed (or stupefied), basically unarmed mob stormed the White House. I saw doors wide open and police standing idly by as they waltzed in. Ashli Babbitt, an unarmed veteran, was shot and killed by a plainclothes officer. The government elite's reaction to the storming of the White House was so swift and fierce that there was no chance for any retaliation. Good Lord, man, if they had been so inspired when people were rioting all throughout the summer, many lives, businesses, and homes would have been saved. No one seemed to care about the veteran that was killed for no apparent reason. The blatant hypocrisy of both parties is appalling at best.

I believe the country will hit the worst recession since the Great Depression. This will trigger the pendulum to swing the other way, and there will be a wave of conservatism that has not been seen in this country for many years. Whatever the future may hold, Carol and I decided we needed to take a vacation before Biden initiated new lockdown measures. That meant another vacation.

Suicide and San Lucas

Pandemic rule #10.5 It is only a day in a life

My wife has always said that if a person could just see that whatever the issue is that is making them want to kill themselves, *it's only a day in a life.*

It's all quite ludicrous, you know. We all know that we'll eventually die. Very few of us know when or how, but the fact that we as human beings will each extinguish at some point or another is undeniable. Whether one wishes to acknowledge it, or not, knowing this fact, knowing that our very existences are but ephemeral flashes upon this earth, we still choose to live as if we have all the time in the world. I'm sure it's our design, our programming, that allows us to comfortably move along in a semi-straight path, always headed slowly toward our end, yet thinking very little about it until death's shadow is looming over us and we can no longer ignore its existence.

What's so ludicrous about it is the fact that we know our lives are fleeting, yet we spend so much time doing things we don't really want to do. I'm not talking about making the bed, brushing your teeth or cleaning up your dog's poo, either. If you knew you had one week to live, how would you spend that week? Why wait until that week is upon us to do that which we most want to do? Hey, I get it, people can't be running around with toilet paper dangling out of their asses just because they feel like they don't have time to properly wipe. Okay, maybe that's a shitty way to put it, but you get the point, right? We have to take time to do the mundane tasks in life in order to survive. But why do we conform with so little for so long knowing our time is so limited? Why do we drive so much to get to work, missing our children's events so we can make some overtime, or waste two hours of our lives watching other people live their lives on social media?
I know, when you started reading this book it was light-hearted. Maybe you even found it funny. I had no intention of it getting this deep. But how can we belly-laugh at a Dave

Chapelle/Joe Rogan (thanks Ben!) show if we
haven't experienced the deep pain of loss or
suffering? How can there be highs without lows?
How would life exist if there was no death? This
is precisely why I'm up at two in the morning
writing this book that perhaps no one will ever
read. This is why Carol and I decided to take a
week and a half and fly to San Lucas during the
pandemic, despite the tragic event that occurred
just a few hours before we were scheduled to
leave.

Suicide and San Lucas will be literally linked
together now and for me can never be
dismantled. Certain events, however unrelated,
become related in a person's mind because of
simple sequence. The sweet smell of a rose
reminds someone of the last time they saw their
grandma. The scent of cookies baking reminds
another of their childhood. For me, San Lucas
and its mysterious rocks and starry skies will
always be tied to a young man's suicide.

Thursday morning, I was standing in the
bathroom, looking in the mirror and deciding
whether or not to go to the gym before we flew
out to Cabo San Lucas, when I heard my
neighbor screaming. Her terror was such that I
knew at once whatever had happened was going

to be very bad. Still, I would not be prepared for the sight that I was about to behold. I put on sweats and told my wife to call 911. I ran out to find my neighbor's teenage son against the tree in their front yard, his mother, my neighbor, screaming and holding him. I saw a white extension cord around his neck. Another neighbor, from the other side of her house, was standing there and asked me to get a knife to cut him down. I went back inside, found a knife, and went back out to find that they already had the young man on the ground and the other neighbor was performing CPR. I went to his side and assisted him. My neighbor's son's eyes were blank and glassy. He still had some warmth to his cheeks, but in my heart, I knew from the second I saw him that he was gone. Still, this young Mexican man and I continued CPR until the ambulance arrived in what seemed like a miniature eternity, all the while my poor neighbor was screaming, her sanity temporarily aflight. Her young man, now eternally young, had some breath come out of him. I'm sure that my neighbor's and my efforts were probably in vain because the child's brain was long gone. If we had to do it again, though, we would. A chance, any chance, is worth a life.

Carol and I tried to keep her calm while the paramedics were working on her boy. He was tall, affable, and I remembered him going after my dog when she got loose on more than one occasion. We even played ball once or twice outside the house. I can't say we're incredibly close to our neighbors, but we're friendly, and, like all good Americans, we all look out for each other. That, to me, is the best type of neighbor. Carol, ever in mama-mode, remained calm and looked after people – our neighbor's kids and their mom. My neighbor's mother and siblings showed up to take care of their family. The paramedics got the neighbor's son into the ambulance, and we went back to our house after ensuring the rest of the kids were okay.

After the ambulance had finally left, and the detective came, I knew the boy had not made it. I went to tell my other neighbor that he had done a good job, but he had left for work. I don't know if he had any formal training or not, but I can tell you from experience, even people who do have training often freeze up in situations like this. As I mentioned, he is Mexican, my neighbor is black and my family is a mix. I made a point to say this because we live in a typical Texas suburb and no one gave a shit about anyone else's race, or politics; we all came together as Americans often do just because it is the right thing.

The sound of my wife's voice brought me back to her. "Should we cancel our trip?"

I looked at my wife. I had also thought about cancelling our trip to Los Cabos. I didn't know what we could possibly do for our neighbor that the family wouldn't do for her better. Honestly, in one singularly traumatic moment, the trip meant nothing to me or Carol. I just wanted to seek out my kids and hug them. Staying home and watching our neighbor's people come and go, and us awkwardly waiting for that moment when we could approach her, well, it didn't seem like that was the best option.

"No, there's no point. What are we going to do by being here?"

Carol agreed. Was that callous or selfish? Perhaps, but we've always been pragmatic. As I said, we're not that close to our neighbor. Our hanging around wasn't a benefit to her. If we had thought for a second that she would need us in some way that her family wasn't already there to do, we would have scrapped the trip without a second thought. I've lost a child, as well. My ex-wife and I practically raised her youngest brother who was nine when we married. Omar was a hard-working, life-loving kid that was more man at a very young age than most men would ever hope to be. He raised a lot of hell, but he always took care of his family. He died of cancer at twenty-three years of age. His death was the catalyst that caused me to decide to change my life.

I believe that one's best option is to live life to its fullest in honor of those who have departed. That philosophy drives me to write, take vacations, and cook out as often as I can for our kids. We would leave, on our flight, and I would call all of my kids, and we would continue on. But drinks were definitely in order.

The flight to San Jose was uneventful. The plane was barely half-full. Most Americans are not traveling much during this, the end of year one of the pandemic lockdowns. It's sad to lose someone you care for, regardless of the circumstances. I don't believe masks have "flattened the curve," nor have the restrictions on restaurants and bars, nor shutting down schools. The rate of deaths stayed pretty steady from May until November. From November until presently (February 2021), they've risen steadily. Some will argue the death rates have increased due to decreased restrictions. New York and California still have the highest death rates, although I'm sure those two states had the strictest restrictions of just about any other state. Texas is third. Florida, the state that had the least COVID restrictions, has nearly half as many deaths as New York. By the way, populations in these states are in the following order, most to least – California, Texas, Florida, then New York. I'm no mathematician, but these numbers based on what the government has been spouting since March of 2020 don't seem to add up. I still believe the restrictions actually worsened the pandemic by not allowing the spread to occur naturally, thereby not reaching herd immunity, as well as forcing people to stay indoors more (furthering a lack of vitamin D), making them more susceptible to the virus. That's right, the doctor, Dr. Paxton, that is, is in.

After landing, Carol and I rented a car and drove to the first resort of three we would eventually stay at. The people in Mexico tend to wear their masks everywhere, even walking outside and driving. Mexico also has the third highest death rate in the world at the time I'm writing this book. We were warmly greeted at the resort, an all-inclusive deal. Our neighbor's death was still very much in the forefront of our minds, so we got some drinks and wound down a bit in the room. We had a lovely seafood dinner and a few more drinks. As the sun set, a cover band played outside of the lobby. A bonfire was in front of the group, and we sat down around it and listened.

We met a young man and his mother. At first, we had both thought she was his sugar mama, until we saw him the next day with his wife as well. He was drinking an Old Fashioned, and I was impressed because it is a drink that I rarely see young people have. We talked for a while, and they left. A young, drunk couple showed up and we talked with them. They said there was a night club around the corner on the property that was open, and they'd check it out and come get us if it was true. They never showed back up. Soon another mother/son pair arrived on the scene, and we spoke with them. They were Greek. Mom had nice legs. I was pretty drunk, and I talked about what had happened earlier that day. The young man spoke of a friend who he had lost to suicide. Later, after the band had left and the bonfire gathering was winding down, the young man told me I was a "sexy mother fucker" in front of his quite appalled mother. Or maybe he said old mother fucker. Whatever.

The next day, while waiting in line for a most delicious cappuccino, we saw the New York couple. Indeed, they had danced. They had been the only ones in the club and forgot to go get us, sorry, blah blah. We told them we'd go that night. I decided to ensure a successful night at the club, so as we met other couples, we told them about the night club and invited basically everyone. At nine that night, Carol and I found the club empty. There was a karaoke style DJ booth and music was playing, but there was no one there. Not even a bartender. I would not be deterred and went to the front desk, flirting while simultaneously demanding a DJ and a bartender for the empty club. I went to the lobby bar and ordered drinks. There was another couple at the bar and I invited them to join. A couple who had joined us for dinner (they had talked to us like we had known each other, a case of mistaken identity, or I met them while drunk, not sure which) also showed up. We had an amazing time. We repeated it the next night.

Carol and I are in our fifties. We love to dance. While we respect others' right to shelter at home and do what they believe to be safe, we don't subscribe to putting life on hold for a virus that is not nearly as deadly as initially thought, especially after we both had it already. I'm sure you've already figured that out by now.

A few days later, we went to the second resort, Pueblo Bonito. We had seven nights booked there. I want to highlight our adventures from this amazing place.

- Our balcony view was of the beach and ocean. We watched whales from the comfort of our room.
- We walked our asses off. The resort has golf carts that take people up and down steep hills all day and night, but we opted to walk ninety-five percent of the time.
- We had three pool options. If we were lazy, we could go to the pool in front of our room. If we wanted to socialize and have immediate access to the beach, we went to a pool right off the beach. If we wanted to have an amazing view, we went to a pool on top of the mountain. The sunset from there was breathtaking.
- I'm in school again (a veteran benefit I decided to take advantage of) and was able to do all my homework and testing and papers from the balcony with an ocean view.
- We danced and met people four of seven nights. Even though we're old, twenty and thirty somethings were always hanging around us. We were the cool kids.
- We both got hit on by younger people more than once.
- Random people bought us liquor the whole time we were there.

-	Whenever people found out about our prior service, they thanked us in such a genuine and real way, it made us both uncomfortable as well as proud.
-	We got amazing thirty-dollar full body massages almost every other day.
-	We ate a lot of fresh seafood.
-	We met really cool people from all over the United States.
-	I gave my cowboy hat to a waiter because he loved it so much, and it only cost me twenty-five dollars at a gas station. It made his week, and I had a good reason to buy a new hat.

Pandemic rule # 11- The locals know the best restaurants and the coolest stories, so talk to them

I kept telling Carol about how we needed to take a trip to Todos Santos. For some reason, it kept getting put off. Ugh, I'm getting ahead of myself again. On check out day at the second resort, we had until three p.m. to check in at the new hotel. A few days earlier, we had decided on a whim to stay a few more days, and I was able to get us a suite at yet another resort – it was a steal. American Airlines has always treated us superbly, and they changed the tickets to Thursday without issues.

Carol had been wanting to go on an excursion. I can't believe that woman isn't satisfied with just eating, drinking, dancing and the beach!

As we drove to the new hotel (early so we could get check-in done and leave our stuff there), we noticed a sign to "Wild Canyon Adventures." We had seen this sign all over buses in San Lucas, and we decided to drive into the canyon and see what it was all about. Keep in mind, we were driving a rented Chevrolet Spark. The road to the canyon was dirt and a lot of areas were very loose. For many years I've been driving over areas I shouldn't with cars that weren't built to go over them. I sped over the looser areas, took care on the turns, and got us to the top.

What I love about Los Cabos is not just the sea, but the stark contrast of the desert that leads up to the coast. The rock formations, the varied type of cacti, and the meeting of the Pacific with the Gulf of California make the area unique. The entire land formation was under water millions of years ago and marine fossils can be found all over. Imagine the Spanish conquistadors' awe while exploring the desert "wasteland" and suddenly coming upon the vastness of the ocean. Many pirates had made the area home, at least temporarily, due to its remoteness. And now they have been replaced by Californians.

We did not stay at the canyon for long. We took pictures and explored the area prior to arriving at the ziplines and horseback riding. I'm not big on the touristy type of attractions, so we left and eventually made it to our third resort. Our suite had a jacuzzi on top of the room, and our view was breathtaking. We drank, met people, and ate. We watched a dance show and danced ourselves. Everything shut down by eleven, because everyone knows COVID-19 is much more contagious after midnight (easy brah, sarcasm not misinformation).

We got up early the next day and drove to Todos Santos. The drive was beautiful and clear. The clouds in the sky were painted by the sunrise, hues of red, orange, and purple. We drove along the coast for many miles, all the while marveling at the fact that the area has still not become completely commercialized. Shortly before arriving at Todos Santos, we stopped at a small town called El Pescadero. There we had the most amazing sourdough-type bread at a tiny coffee shop and bakery called Le Petit, which is located next to a convenience store called OXXO. The owner is a man from France. If you're ever in the area, I highly recommend you have any of their baked goods and an expresso.

"Okay, babe, you're in store for a little surprise."

"Really? What?" Carol cast a suspicious look towards me.

"You know, the song Hotel California was actually a hotel."

"Yes, I know that."

"Well, you're about to see it."

That's right. The actual Hotel California from the song is in Baja California. It was built in 1948 by a Chinese immigrant named Mr. Wong. Except it's an urban legend. Apparently, this "haunted" hotel has nothing to do with the song. But the song did make the little hotel a famous stopping spot for all things gringo. I had not known this fact when I originally spoke with Carol about the hotel. I don't want anyone getting the "Wong" idea.

Todos Santos has been overrun by gringo hipsters. Father Bravo, the founder of the mission that later became the town, would probably SMH about that all day (boomer translation notation – SMH means shakin' my head). Fishing was the town's primary source of commerce for many years. We had an amazing breakfast at Caffe Todos Santos (I loved the chilaquiles and the fresh orange juice). After taking a tour of the hotel, we headed to Punta Lobos, a small fishing cove just a few minutes from Todos Santos. Years ago, I had gone fishing on a small boat just off this very cove. When we arrived, however, what I found was a very different looking cove.

The small cove had changed significantly since I had last been there. A fancy resort sat overlooking the cove, the fishing boats in plain sight. We parked in an area designated for the fishermen and beach visitors and walked down to where twenty or so fishing boats were strewn about on the beach. A man was cleaning his boat as I approached him. His name was Eugenio Nunez, and he was a fourth-generation fisherman. After some initial pleasantries, I told him it had been over ten years since I had been here and asked him about the resort. He had a lot to say about it.

"Do you remember how it was here the last time you came?"

"That resort wasn't here. It was all trees."

"Yes. One day, they showed up, and within weeks this hotel was here. Then, the owners decided they didn't want us fishing here anymore."

"So, some non-locals buy a piece of land next to a cove where fishing has been the way of life for decades, and they decide that because your boats are an eyesore that y'all need to fish elsewhere?"

"That's it. They wouldn't let us through to the cove, so we all got together and protested outside of the hotel. That morning – it was still dark – dozens of police, federal and state, came out and arrested us all."

"Was there any violence?"

"You know how it is with police in Mexico."

I nodded. My run-ins with federal police while investigating some executions and missing women in Juarez for my book *The Plaza* had been unpleasant, to say the least.

"Some of the fishermen got hurt. A lawyer decided to help us and got us all out of jail. He later was jailed, too. The police had sided with the hotel and everything was against us. All of

Todos Santos got involved when they jailed the lawyer and protested until they let him out."

"So, in the end, y'all are still here."

"We're still here. They are, too. But now we just leave each other alone."

Progress is a precarious. She's also a capricious bitch. Progress hurts feelings, but it doesn't always have to. This story gets better.
Back at the resort, at a seafood-themed buffet, my wife and I started chatting with a young lady who was asking for reviews on our resort stay. She was from Todos Santos, and we talked with her about Nunez's story.

"The resort came with all sorts of hope and promises. A university would be built in Todos Santos, providing the area with education, courses in English, and opportunities to stay in Todos Santos and have some kind of future."

She corroborated the fisherman's story. I assumed this university was a Mexican university. I was wrong.

Later research uncovered some interesting facts. A large amount of land had once been donated to

Colorado State University. A lot of acreage. And they either sold it or made a partnership with a real estate investment company called MIRA that had a lot of U.S. investment money. This land that was donated to the university for "research" was now being developed for tourism. We're in the wrong business.

Chapter Twelve- A Freeze and Funds for Felons

Pandemic Rule # 12- Don't underestimate the importance of firewood

We got back home at the end of January. My neighbor had cut the tree in front of her house down. Carol and I went to pay our respects. She was grateful for what we had tried to do. We hugged and cried. I had no words for her. There is no worse pain to feel than the loss of a child. We were relieved to have spoken with her.

When the Texas freeze hit, we were unprepared. There was no excuse for me not prepping. Having firewood and a generator ready to go in the winter is common sense. Having extra water is common sense. Having plenty of canned foods at hand, and beer, and liquor, is common sense. We have seen shortages in Texas now from several disasters and the pandemic. We already know people panic shop, but all we had was liquor.

The first day temperatures got below thirty and the snow actually stuck. We went sliding down the hills at a nearby park with my youngest son and his cousin.

The next day, we woke up to a power outage. By noon, I knew the crap the electric company was spewing about a rolling outage and it being only for a few hours at a time was bullshit. We made sure our neighbors were good, and we abandoned ship. We drove to the local casino where we had "free" rooms for a few days. Shockingly, I had a few too many drinks and did some writing. I've included it, unedited:

Drunk Writing

Texas just got hit with mild Minnesota weather, and it shut down power grids and cell phone towers. The windmill farms fuckin' froze. We haven't had electricity since early this morning. We are supposed to be taking a break from casinos, but they are currently offering warmth and internet. I knocked on my neighbor's door and asked if they were good. Yes, my neighbor with a bunch of kids that her boy recently committed suicide. She is an amazing woman. She's keeping her shit together. I don't think I would. I lost one kid (not biological, but helped raise him) and if I ever have the terrible misfortune to lose another, I don't think I'll make it sanely. But she is holding up. There are like six kids living there, and they had cereal. The hell with it, I'm grilling for them all. I pulled out ribeye and chicken from our fridge. Carol helped me prep and I cooked it all and gave it to them. I kept a ribeye for us. I remember in the military how much warm meals meant when you had been in the field. I figure it's the same for a bunch of kids dealing with cold. All that ribeye would just contribute to the delinquency of our fat cells anyway.

We're at the casino. It has electricity and internet. I haven't ventured down to the casino yet because I was fucking around with my Spotify and writing. Carol went down and now is back up in the room and is going to rest. I'm about to head down and honestly, I'll probably continue drinking because this seems like a good night stay inebriated. I had a dream the other day where I was holding my neighbor's son in my arms and was looking at his face and his lifeless eyes and hearing my neighbor scream a scream that only a mother screams when her baby dies. I'm about to have a few more drinks. Don't get me wrong, I know that this is just an excuse to drink. I choose to drink tonight, not use my anxiety as a crutch. I just want to get hammered.

I forgot I had written this. It was deeper than I thought. I'm including this because it is honest and as you probably figured out this book is more like a journal than anything else. Thank you, dear reader, for being my unwitting therapist.

The freeze is over. Temperatures are returning to "Texas" normal. Stimulus has been passed. Little of it had to do with true stimulus. Did you know convicts in jail are getting stimulus money, too? They have to apply for it, but are eligible. Your friendly neighborhood child molester can get government cheese as well as the hard-working single mom can. I could go on and on about all of the other bullshit that went into the bill. There are people pushing for a fifteen-dollar minimum wage. Some companies have already opted to close down stores or automate instead of paying more people a higher wage. I have a suggestion. Instead of paying millions of dollars to foreign governments for God-only-knows-what, we could subsidize companies to pay higher wages. Instead of flooding the country with cheap labor (yes, the hundreds of immigrants who are crossing daily and getting bus tickets to their new home, and stimulus too!), we could pay our own countrymen more. Seems reasonable to me, but someone who reads this will probably call me a racist or an asshole, or both.

Chapter Thirteen- Dr. Seuss – Get a Noose

Pandemic Rule # 13- Yesterday's fable is tomorrow's example of racism and should be destroyed and forgotten forever

Texas has removed the mandatory mask mandate. As you know, I've never been a fan of the mask. Many people forgot when our "top" doctor, Fauci, said on television that masks are relatively ineffective. Judging by the high infection rates that have plagued the country during the mandatory masks and social distancing, I think he actually said the truth back then. I do believe what was said early on that people who are actively coughing and sick should wear a mask. It doesn't do a lot of good, but at least everyone would know who to socially distance from. All my life I've hated sitting on the plane close to someone hacking their lungs out. Remember the flu? The flu has put me on my ass more than a few times.

By the way, did you know that Dr. Seuss was a racist? Let's ban his books. God forbid our children learn from the racist words of Dr. Seuss who spoke about the different characters being more similar than they thought and not making fun of each other for differences in appearances. As far as the "racist" images, well, let's really take a look at sketches on SNL and the Dave Chapelle Show and see if we don't see any examples of stereotyping of any race ever. I wonder if the same parents who are upset over Dr. Seuss are upset about the many contemporary songs that liberally use the "N" word in the hook, or talk about the wetness of their pussy, or violence against others. Or how about the TV shows that promote promiscuity? I'm no puritan. I'm okay with some nudity, and there is a lot of rap songs that I like that would definitely be on the rated "mature" level. I'm also not hypocritically looking to ban the things I simply decide that I don't like for whatever reason. One thing I do not want or tolerate is for people to teach my children that our country is racist, and they're inherently racist if they are white, and successful black people are a "one-off." Am I naïve enough to believe racism doesn't exist in the USA? Of course not. Racism – it's not just for white people anymore.

I once rode in an Uber with a man who told me he was racist. He was black. He told me he did not and would not hang around with white people, and he sure as hell didn't like them. He spoke at length as to why white people could not be trusted and that their inferiority to black people was the very reason that they created laws and systems to undermine the black race. While I appreciated his candor, he was clearly a racist by both the old as well as the new definition of racist. Unless you're a follower of the critical race theory in which case his racism was justified and thereby nullified. By the way, you might think that I reported the racist Uber driver or didn't tip him, but that would be incorrect. I gave him a good rating and a regular tip because he was honest about the way he felt. Even if a person is clearly wrong on a point or belief that they have, I respect them if they are willing to talk about it despite whom it may offend.

I also believe people are innocent until proven guilty. I refuse to defend myself against any charge of racism. If you want to call me a racist, that's your prerogative and right, but I'm innocent until you prove otherwise. The burden of proof should always be on the accuser, not the accused.

Chapter Fourteen- Vaccinate – and wear two masks!

Pandemic Rule # 14- For instructions, see option A.

A.   See option B.
B.   See option A, then refer to C.
C.   Refer to Dr. Fauci's statement Not that one, the one before that.

D.   Awww, fuck it.

The Coronavirus has been used to destroy people and their reputations. It has been used to divide us as a nation. And its effects are as profound as they are enduring. The guy who doesn't feel safe in public and wants to double-mask even after he has been vaccinated is well within his rights. The lady who refuses to wear a mask and refuses to vaccinate is also within her rights. Yet, the rise of the scientist-politician has ruined our tolerance for one another. Now, every Tom, Dick, and Dr. Fauci have an opinion on what the public should do or how they should feel depending on their particular political affiliation. Science should be based on testing, math, and facts, not emotion. If we as a nation are not allowed to be in public places without a mask even after vaccination, what is the point of vaccination? Other countries that have less of a political interest in the virus have done numerous studies both disproving the mask as a true deterrent of the virus and that vaccinated people being carriers of the virus or being adversely affected by variants is minute at best. The point of vaccination is to improve the vaccinated person's immunity to the virus and bring the country and world to herd immunity. Or so the politicians and scientists have said.

Fauci is a natural politician. He speaks out of both sides of his mouth at the same time. In one breath, he tells us how important it is to vaccinate and without skipping a beat he tells us to wear double masks. He tells us not to travel, and he and Biden say, maybe, just maybe, we can have small, socially distanced gatherings by July the fourth if only we all get vaccinated. Please help me, someone, by use of a logical, fact-based argument, understand these unclear, mixed messages. No maskers! Face diaper wearers! But I think we can solve this classification issue once and for all. If you do not vaccinate or wear a mask, clearly, you're a racist. And if you do wear a mask, even after vaccinating, well, you're a sheep. Or you're on a commercial flight.

Chapter Fifteen-The Disorder at the Border

I really wish I had coined that phrase. Let us put into perspective how the Biden administration is handling the pandemic, the incredible "surge" of illegal immigrants to the border, and his own countrymen. Remember when Biden used the word "surge" as he suggested undocumented immigrants cross the border illegally? Don't believe me? It's all on video. Yeah, "surge" was a big deal on TV for half a second. Then, like many of the terms that offend us, it no longer mattered and we moved onto the next offensive term of the day.

Carol and I are flying to Cancun. In order for us to fly back, we must present negative COVID-19 tests. Yet hundreds of undocumented people have been crossing the border without legal identifications and certainly no COVID tests. Crime in Mexico and Central America has risen steadily since Biden was elected, and these same countries that have the greatest "surges" of their people leaving their countries to dangerously cross crime-ridden borders and treacherous landscapes to hopefully cross the United States border. Even if you as an American don't care about the economic implications of this "surge," you should at least care about the humanitarian aspect. Crossing any border illegally is dangerous. Multiply that by two or even more. Add in deserts, rivers, and dangerous mudslides. If you don't think that deterring parents from sending their ten and twelve-year-old unaccompanied to the United States border is humane, then I really don't know what world you're from. And the entire family crossing together is not much safer.

The problem with illegal immigration has been the same issue for decades. Most illegal immigrants start out desperate in their own countries and are simply looking for a better way of life. No one with any kind of a heart would have a problem understanding this. But allowing them, or worse yet, inviting them to cross by the thousands illegally, is the most inhumane act that any politician could do regarding this issue. We should be continuing what Trump started, and take it to the next level, by forming economic agreements with our neighbors that are mutually beneficial and that will help our neighbors make their countries more appealing to the economically disadvantaged. Helping our neighbors create safer places to live is a direct approach to resolving their crisis. Economy and safety typically go hand in hand.

Chapter sixteen- The End of Highway 666

Pandemic Rule # 16- *You Do You, Let Me Do Me, It's Okay If We Disagree, That's The Beauty of Liberty*

I think that no matter what side of the political spectrum you, dear reader, is on, we must agree that the pandemic has been a real bitch. For those who have lost friends and family during these troubled times because of sickness, violence, or suicide, it was a hellish time. Media's focus seems always to be about anger and negativity. No matter who you are, it's easy to get caught up in it. We're constantly bombarded by the media, via news, social, and otherwise, through stories designed to elicit an emotional response out of us. Anger is usually the easiest to provoke and the most commonly sought after by the media.

There is a guy at my gym who is always side-eyeing me. I swear I can see him looking down at me, even though he is a few inches shorter. He is wearing a mask; I am not. He stays well away from me. In reality, I have no idea what he is really thinking, but his expressions remind me of how others have used mask-wearing and social distancing as ways to elevate themselves, much as I saw people all my life that would use religion as a way to be "better" than others. It's a shame that the focus is often hypocritical rather than genuine concern. And this example also shows how assumptions can be far from the truth. Maybe the gym guy is just watching my form, or thinks I lift too heavy (or too light) of weights. I'm not in his head, so why should I pretend to be? What gives me the right to judge his thoughts especially when I can't read his mind?

I really would like to end this piece with something positive. Navigating the pandemic highway has been a very negative experience for most. Some have gotten rich, while others have found new and better ways to conduct business. There are those of us who actually spent time with our children that we never would have had this pandemic not hit. Do any of these positive things take away from the losses of lives or livelihoods? Of course not. That doesn't mean we should dwell on all things negative.

After this book is written, edited, and published, I'm taking a break. I'm turning off the news. I'm shutting down social media. We're going to take some trips with our kids, any of those who can and want to go with us, and we're going to look ahead on a better future. No, I won't bury my head in the sand. When it comes time to vote, I will. When there are issues that I'm passionate about on a local level, I'll participate in making positive changes. But I will not dwell upon the things I cannot change and will instead look to effect beneficial changes on those around me. I hope that since you have made it this far, will do the same. You must have really hated the book, or really liked it, to have come all this way to the end. Or, shit, did you just skip to the end?

A ninety-year-old man in Tecate, Baja California, once told me his secret to longevity. "There is no reason to worry. It's the most unproductive emotion there is. If a problem arises, there are only two outcomes. Either there is a resolution for it, or there is not. Worry is never a means to either outcome. So why worry?"

I thank you for having come to the end of this road with me. I hope, even if you hated some of what I said, that you found something useful or entertaining in this. With any luck, I made you smile at least once. Do yourself a favor. Take my wise old friend's advice. Quit worrying so much about COVID-19, who's wearing a mask and who isn't, or who the next president might be. Turn off the news. Turn on some music you like and envision yourself doing something you love. Then, do it.

Meanwhile, I'll finish up my next novel on a beach, a stout drink in my hand and the smell of carne asada in the breeze...

www.ingramcontent.com/pod-product-compliance
Lightning Source LLC
Chambersburg PA
CBHW070814050426
42452CB00011B/2041